Acknowledgements

This final product is the result of a small group of ladies who exemplify the something about Mary in each of their personal lives. I offer my sincere appreciation to Joy Lower, Bev Herring and Carol Wilson for the respective insights and instruction each woman provided in the formulation of this project. Thank-you ladies, I am honored by your courtesy.

I also want to acknowledge my wife Stacey, my best friend and closest confidante. Stacey, I am thrilled that you are my life-partner.

Dedication

I am dedicating this book to the three most wonderful women in my life; Stacey, my wife, and my two daughters, Spencer and McKinlee. Stacey and McKinlee, you have demonstrated the 'something' about Mary in extraordinary, amazing ways and I have every expectation and belief that you will continue to do so for the rest of your lives. I am excited to see what God has immaculately conceived for you.

I am offering an exclusive dedication to my oldest daughter, Spencer, because she is witnessing the publication of this book from an eternal vantage. A short while before her death, Spencer and I were talking about an idea for a book-one of many ideas for a book I have discussed with my family of women over the years. After I finished telling her the premise, she looked at me and said, "Don't let this one die, Dad".

I remember those words of encouragement and have been haunted by them since her death on September 27, 2010. To honor Spencer and her passion for Christ in every facet of her life, I am adding her name to the dedication page of "The 'SOMETHING' About Mary" and I am publishing the book under the acronym of "TODDS! Publishing".

This **O**ne **D**idn't **D**ie, **S**pencer!
And others are going to live....

Contents

Introduction

'But when the fulness of the time was come, God sent forth his Son, made of a woman, made under the law,'

Galatians 4:4

It is always only in the right moment of time that God sets in motion another part of His plan for humanity. Even though scriptures plainly tell us that Jesus was slain (crucified) from the foundations of the world (Revelation 13:8), many thousands of years came and went before the Man, Jesus physically appeared on the earthly stage in a little, seeming insignificant country, known as Israel. The rest is history and ultimately affects our future, perhaps sooner than anyone of us might suspect.

Time is moving so fast and change happens so quickly with each passing day it appears that modern humanity is ever closer to another one of God's 'fulness of time' events. The 'fulness of time' Paul talked about in Galatians—the arrival of Jesus—is still impacting the world today, even though at that particular time, most all the world's population was unaware of His divine birth. If we are really getting close to a time when God might choose to do something wonderfully impactful, will we know, or will we miss it? Will we seize the opportunity that the moment reveals, or let it pass unseen?

In the following pages, you will be introduced to the young Jewish woman Mary in a different, more human way. We sometimes forget Mary was getting ready to be married when the angel first appeared to her. It would have been totally understandable if she had missed the time for God to send His Son. But she didn't. She was intuitively ready to be a part of God's plan, and what she said and did during her angelic visit proves it.

There are stories of others who were ready for the arrival of Jesus at God's fullness of time. But two of them were old and spent their time in the temple waiting to see the personification of Salvation. There were some shepherds keeping watch over sleeping sheep, who received a special, Heavenly invitation to witness the birth of Jesus and had the common sense to take advantage of a once-in-a-life-time, miraculous event. And most of us are familiar with stories about the wise men that travelled long and far to honor the one born "King of the Jews". All these people were prepared in their respective fashions to herald Jesus at the time of His birth and early life.

But Mary did more than wait, or witness, or travel to view the arrival of Jesus; she *lived* His arrival completely. Mary made the arrival of Jesus and His entire life possible. Mary somehow recognized the 'fullness of time' opportunity God was presenting to her and she made full advantage of the moment. The world is blessed today because of the something about Mary, which can be the something about each of us, as well...if we dare.

Mary's Story: part 1

She was getting extremely tired of always being asked to go to another part of the house whenever Joe came to visit her parents. The handsome carpenter was a well-known and respected businessman in town and he had been coming to see her parents a lot more often than she could remember before. She thought her parents might be getting ready to have something built for them, but wasn't totally convinced.

She liked Joe as far as she knew him and liked him coming around because, even though she would never tell her parents this secret, he was really cute. As she tried to find something to do that would occupy her attention, she could not help but overhear the muffled voices from the other room. The tones were friendly and at times there was loud laughter. She did not completely understand why she was so nervous about conversations she could not really hear, but she knew that plans were being discussed which would affect her life.

Now the back and forth between her parents and Joe were getting louder and more emotional. She thought she heard her mother crying, but wasn't sure, because she still heard laughing too. It was strange. All of the sudden, she heard a loud cheer. Her father and Joe were congratulating one another.

Then she heard her mother calling her name. Something had happened and now the adults wanted Mary to come into the room to be included in the conversation. She wasn't sure she wanted to join them just yet, but she heard a soft knock on her bedroom door and as her mother peeked in and said,

"Mary?...your father and I would like to introduce you to Joseph,...your future husband."

Chapter One

Hello, Mary.

The Adventure Begins

Mention the Virgin Mary anywhere in the world and there is an instant recognition factor. It is universally understood in major parts of the world that Mary gave birth to the most famous son in all of human history; Jesus, the Son of God.

Jesus Christ is the most important and per- haps most controversial figure in human his- tory. If you are in any way curious about his life, you should read the Bible, a book which gives detailed accounts of the miraculous activities done and the bold claims made by Jesus while he lived on the earth. For the 2000 plus years since Jesus lived in Israel, people have debated whether or not this man who claimed to be God's only Son is who he says, or was just some guy who has benefitted from the greatest marketing campaign the earth will ever know.

Imagine that human existence as we know it were to end today. Even if Jesus is not, or cannot possibly be, who he claims to be—the actual Son of God, think about the impact this Jesus has had on civilization since he was born, lived, died, and disappeared to who knows where with the promise of coming again;

> The world marks the calendar which governs days, weeks, months and years by his approximate time of existence; (BC) Before Christ. (AD)Anno Domini-the year of our Lord-after his death.

> The world's largest religious demographic is made up by the people who follow his teachings. Many other world religions recognize Jesus as a prophet or at least a great teacher.

> At least two world-recognized and celebrated holidays are held in his honor or memory; Christmas and Easter.

Wars, both secular and religious, have been initiated in, for or against his name. And combatants on every side of the conflicts have invoked His name in the hope of victory.

Science and scientists, scholars and philosophers are locked in studies and debates trying to prove or disprove him and his deeds, his teachings and his miracles.

Thousands of fiction and non-fiction books and countless other media have been written and produced about his life, his teachings, his miracles, and even his alleged marriage, children and still existent physical descendants.

Miraculously these accomplishments are attributed to a man who left no real tangible evidence of his existence. There are no first-hand writings, no images in stone, metal or period art, no historical monuments, nothing, except devoted followers who still proclaim not just his existence (past and present), but his divinity as well. Jesus Christ is undeniably a lasting and impactful historical and future presence, but this book is not about Him.

This book is about the woman God chose to be His mother, who as a young Israelite woman, agreed to be the surrogate mother of God's own Son, even though she was already engaged to be married to a man named Joseph. In her responsibilities as the mother of Jesus, Mary, who had no formal 'Christian' training, instilled into Jesus the fundamental basis for his human attitudes, behaviors and ability to relate to people at large.

Mary would not have had the benefit of a New Testament construct. All she had ever known or been taught was Old Testament laws and rituals. Only after Christ began His earthly ministry would the concept of God's love be verbalized,...by Jesus. Everything we take for granted in the post-modern age of Christianity would have been totally foreign and perhaps irreligious to Mary's way of processing who, or what God is. Mary had to impart into Jesus, God's Son, a way for Him to make God not terrifying and worth loving and serving.

Interestingly though, the Bible is not all that forthcoming with information about Mary.

Beyond being a virgin woman living in Nazareth and engaged to a man named Joseph there is not much more detail to give the woman Mary any kind of unique individuality. From the few scant facts given in scripture about her it seems as though the benevolent, caring and wise God of creation did not really put a whole lot of thought or care into the character or qualifications of the person who should be the mother of His child. It appears as though He just needed a willing, submissive, naïve girl in whom to incubate a baby and any girl He chose would be 'blessed above all other women'; or in today's lingo, *lucky beyond all belief*.

From everything that has ever been revealed about God and His nature, it is easy and correct to conclude that nothing could be further from God's Truth. An eternity of strategic thought, organizational and logistical planning went into His selection of Mary, the Virgin from Nazareth, to be the mother of Jesus. In fact scripture relates that it was only in "the fullness of the time", or at the exact right moment, when every single one of the wide ranging variables including *people*, were exactly when and where everything and everybody needed to be, that God sent His Son to earth.

There is something that made Mary quite different from other women who might have displayed the diminutive qualities a chauvinistic god would be looking for in a mere baby mama. Imagine for a moment that you are God and you need to find a woman to give birth to and successfully raise your son, the 'Son of God', to adulthood! Not only does the woman you choose have to fit certain physical criteria– by the statements of your own holy messengers, the prophets, she must be a virgin. But, the woman must also be capable of fulfilling any and all parental responsibilities without any real direct physical contact or other discernible interaction by you.

From your 'god-perspective', the child you are asking a single, soon to be married, woman to carry and raise is the purported Savior of the world and will be remembered for millennia after His life is finished on earth. The eternal fate of all humanity and the world rests on her overall success as a surrogate parent. Everything you've planned depends upon the woman you choose! So the woman you 'favored' would need to

possess something very special in her person-
ality make-up and character for you to be able to
trust her with so great a task.

> **Question:** If you were God,
> what would you look for in such
> a woman?

A thorough and honest consideration of
the sheer magnitude of nuance and strategy
involved in such a monumental task would lead
any thoughtful deity to the realization that it is
not really in the best interest of the plan to simply
grab some random virgin girl who just happens
to be living in the right place on the planet at the
right time in the entire history of creation. So...,

> **Second Question:** What would
> <the real> God look for in such
> a woman?

Most certainly the God of all creation, whose
entire plan for saving humanity from an eternity
in hell would rest upon the ability of a woman,
one woman, to ensure His child's survival and
rearing, would have super high standards for
selecting a surrogate. God's standards would
most certainly surpass those of even the most

discerning and demanding prospective earthly parent.

God saw something in the woman Mary that He could not ignore or overlook. She possessed certain qualities and the character necessary to guarantee the success of the Son of God in his mission to bring about eternal life and redemption for all humankind.

To be sure, Mary carried seeds of greatness within her. But contrary to what anyone might think or say about the rest of earth's populace, we all have the seeds of something special and we all have the ability to nurture the growth of it in our lives as well. Why? Because it is not something secret, elusive or unobtainable. Every human being is born with the something about Mary. It is inherent in the very DNA of what makes people special. This is especially true for those who have made Jesus Christ Lord and Master by responding to His free gift of Salvation.

God has made us who believe alive to His nature so during our lifetimes we can bring glory to Him in the earth by doing great things to and for the people who still need to be introduced to an awesome God.

'...for you are a chosen people. You are royal priests, a holy nation, God's very own possession. As a result you can show others the goodness of God, for he called you out of darkness into his wonderful light.'

I Peter 2:9
New Living Translation

This book will explore and explain exactly what God saw in His choice as the mother of His son. So in order to fully understand Mary's journey, we must start where her story begins,

'Now in the sixth month the angel Gabriel was sent by God to a city of Galilee named Nazareth, to a virgin betrothed to a man whose name was Joseph, of the house of David. The virgin's name was Mary. And having come in, the angel said to her, "Rejoice, highly favored one, the Lord is with you; blessed are you among women!" But when she saw him, she was troubled at his saying, and considered what manner of greeting this was. Then the angel said to her, "Do not be afraid, Mary, for you have found favor with God.

"And behold, you will conceive in your womb and bring forth a Son, and shall call His name JESUS." He will be great, and will be called the Son of the Highest; and the Lord God will give Him the throne of His father David. "And He will reign over the house of Jacob forever, and of His kingdom there will be no end." Then Mary said to the angel, "How can this be, since I do not know a man?" And the angel answered and said to her, "The Holy Spirit will come upon you, and the power of the Highest will overshadow you; therefore, also, that Holy One who is to be born will be called the Son of God." Now indeed, Elizabeth your relative has also conceived a son in her old age; and this is now the sixth month for her who was called barren. "For with God nothing will be impossible." Then Mary said, "Behold the maidservant of the Lord! Let it be to me according to your word." And the angel departed from her. Now Mary arose in those days and went into the hill country with haste, to a city of Judah, and entered the house of Zacharias and greeted Elizabeth. And it happened, when Elizabeth heard the greeting of Mary, that the babe leaped in her womb; and Elizabeth was filled with the Holy Spirit. Then she spoke out with a loud voice and said, "Blessed are you among women, and blessed is the fruit of your womb! "But why is this granted to me, that the mother of my Lord should come to me? "For indeed, as soon as the voice of your greeting sounded in my ears, the babe leaped in my womb for joy. "Blessed is she who believed, for there will be a fulfillment of those things which were told her from the Lord." And Mary said: "My soul magnifies the Lord, and my spirit has rejoiced in God my Savior. For He has regarded the lowly state of His maidservant; for behold, henceforth all generations will call me blessed. For He who is mighty has done great things for me, and holy is His name. And His mercy is on those who fear Him from generation to generation. He has shown strength with His arm; He has scattered the proud in the imagination of their hearts. He has put down the mighty from their thrones, and exalted the lowly. He has filled the hungry with good things, and the rich He has sent away empty. He has helped His servant Israel, in remembrance of His mercy, As He spoke to our fathers, to Abraham and to his seed forever." And Mary remained with her about three months, and returned to her house.'

Luke 1:26-56
New King James Version

In these thirty verses of the gospel of Luke there are six truths which reveal and define the 'something' God saw in Mary which qualified her to carry and raise the Son of God, the Savior of mankind, the King of kings. Imagine the potential and power of a person who determines to cultivate these simple truths into his or her life for the good of all.

The world certainly does not need another savior, but it does need people who can live for the availability of God's purposes for humanity. As you read, allow God to develop the 'something about Mary' inside you.

Mary's Story: part II

Mary was in a mild state of shock. The only thing going over and over in her head was what seemed to her to be a totally off the wall miracle; she was engaged to Joseph! How awesome was that! He was a smart, talented, skilled, well-off carpenter and he was so good looking! She could not have been happier in her current situation. Her parents had made an awesome selection for her and she was glad Joseph was interested in getting married to her out of all the available women in Nazareth.

WOW,....she was going to be married and very soon a new life adventure was about to begin as the wife of Joseph. She experienced one of those rare, 'everything's so unbelievable' shivers down her back. She offered up a quick thanks to God for her recent and many blessings.

In the days since her parents had announced her engagement and introduced her to Joseph, Mary had been reviewing the major events in her life. She acknowledged that up to now hers had been a rather favored and blessed life. While she was certainly not from the richest, most prestigious family in her hometown, her parents had wide respect in the neighborhood and the community. It certainly helped increase her family's standing in town when news that Zacharias, a close relative who was a priest in Jerusalem, had been selected to burn the ritual incense in the temple.

Because Zacharias and his wife Elizabeth, Mary's cousin, had not been able to have children of their own, Mary had developed an unusually close and special relationship with them through the years. She loved the times when she could visit them in the big city of Jerusalem and she was always excited when Zacharias and Elisabeth could make the trip to Nazareth. She smiled as she recalled the many good times both families had shared through the years.

She was so lost in her thoughts that she barely registered the bright light out of the corner of her eye. She turned in amazement while the light grew ever brighter and what looked to be a person, appeared in the middle of the overwhelming whiteness.

'Hello, Mary,' said the imposing figure, 'you are a very favored young woman because the Lord is with you. You are blessed above all other women.'

Mary just stared in wide-eyed wonder and mind-numbed amazement as the majestic figure in the fast-fading light introduced himself as Gabriel, an angel sent from Heaven by God himself. The angel was saying something about God wanting her to be the mother of the Messiah, but she was not hearing anything beyond that, as his words just trailed off into space...she was favored and blessed!

Chapter Two

Accept God's Blessing of Favor

'Now in the sixth month the angel Gabriel was sent by God to a city of Galilee named Nazareth, to a virgin betrothed to a man whose name was Joseph, of the house of David. The virgin's name was Mary. And having come in, the angel said to her, "Rejoice, highly favored one, the Lord is with you; blessed are you among women!" But when she saw him, she was troubled at his saying, and considered what manner of greeting this was. Then the angel said to her, "Do not be afraid, Mary, for you have found favor with God."'

Luke 1: 26-30
New King James Version

f Mary was anything like the majority of women who become engaged to be married, she was probably so completely wrapped up in making plans for her big day that little or nothing else had opportunity to break into her thought process. She would most likely have been excited, nervous and worried about the upcoming marriage ceremony and celebration. Mary would have been intent on ensuring that everything associated with her once-in-a-lifetime wedding went 'just right'.

In other words, she would have been preoccupied with the current events of her life. Her dreams, her plans, her fiancé, her family and friends, everything would have been working against her ability to hear from God about His plan and purpose for her life. Her life, in the context where we are introduced to her, resounds with a very 21st century chaos influenced familiarity. In spite of her busy-ness, the time for God's plan was ripe and circumstances had conveniently, coincidentally and creatively come together into a perfect God-opportunity. And God needed Mary to do Him a favor. God also had to get her undivided attention so He sent an angel to deliver His message.

The angel Gabriel said hello in dramatic fashion, but Mary did not seem to be totally surprised by his appearance, even though she was troubled by what he said,

> Be glad and happy because God thinks you are special and the Lord is with you; you are the most fortunate woman on the planet.

Like most women after hearing an opening line like that, Mary was skeptical and wondered what the angel really wanted. The angel had to reassure her that everything was all right and that she could trust him.

Gabriel went on to say,

> Don't be scared or worried, Mary, God favors you and you are going to become pregnant with a Son, God's Son. And you will name him Jesus.

The angel then explained how great Jesus would be and how he would rule as a king and change the world....Mary had an angel in her house and he was speaking to her about a plan God had–for her–to do Him–a favor. He wanted to 'bless' her by getting her pregnant because He 'favored' her. Yeah, right! With a blessing and favor like that, a newly engaged woman doesn't need too many other enemies or curses in order to derail any good dreams or plans she might have for future married bliss.

This encounter, however, is an important key to understanding a tidbit of the 'something' God saw in Mary. She had to recognize and come to terms with the fact that she was favored and blessed in spite of how that 'favor and blessing' might take shape.

The story clearly states that Mary was troubled by what the angel said to her. The angel told her God favored her and wanted to bless her more than any other woman on earth at that time. Then the angel explained the nature of the 'blessing'-getting pregnant by someone other than her fiancé.

After hearing all this, Mary did not get indignant or ask the angel to leave. She did not accuse the angel of being completely insane to even suggest such a thing, afterall she was a virgin; an engaged virgin, thank-you very much!

Mary surely knew she would be risking her life so she was rightfully skeptical about the proposal–a plan that even on a good day would be tricky to pull off–a plan that would call into question her integrity, her reputation, her spirituality and her sanity.

Yet, she recognized that in the middle of this strange, fantastically divine encounter, she was favored! Her life had a destiny and a purpose beyond merely the wife of a guy named Joe. She was pronounced to be favored and blessed–above the norm–by an angel sent from Heaven. No matter how outrageous it appeared or sounded to anyone else who knew her or might hear of her uniquely improbable situation, she understood that she, Mary, was BLESSED!

Mary not only recognized and acknowledged that she was favored and blessed, she also accepted that reality without reservation. Mary silently, consciously agreed with and believed what the angel told her–that among all other women she was blessed. Mary allowed that statement to permeate her mind, her soul and her spirit. She accepted the idea, notion and concept of the very beautiful blessing and understood its meaning clearly. And she was fine with it!

She could have very easily insisted to Gabriel, 'Oh no, you have the wrong girl. Suzie down the street is much more blessed than me. Her family has more money and status. She is more friendly, better educated and beautiful too. She is so much more deserving than me! I'm not the girl you want, go ask her.' But she did not!

Had Mary said anything to the angel Gabriel that deflected or deferred his proclamation, the angel, who had been sent to Mary by God personally, would have been unable to go on to the next phase of his God-given mission; getting her to do a favor for God.

Many times in life we are presented with absolutely wild opportunities, ideas or plans which we immediately discount because we fail to recognize the blessing and favor of God hidden within the proposition. Beyond the overwhelming probability that God would want to utilize mere humans like us in His plans, we don't even begin to consider the thought as possible because we don't think or feel we are worthy or capable of seeing what God would ask of us all the way through to a successful conclusion.

Yeah, but Mary is different! She was visited by an angel. She was asked to carry God's Son. God got her pregnant. We aren't that important or vital to humanity's future. Wrong! We have all been created for a unique and special purpose that we alone have the strength, ability, talent and divine power to carry out.

If we don't get the profoundness of the idea that we are at least 'as blessed as Mary' locked into our minds and spirits, everything else is just religious psycho-babble and cheap parlor tricks. This is the truth; God asked Mary to do Him a favor and that is the level to which she was favored. You are favored because God created you to do Him a favor; live your life for His glory. Let's put this into a more modern context.

Imagine that you have an important project to complete with a very time-critical deadline. Everything is riding upon the successful completion of the project; your reputation, your credibility and most importantly any future success you might achieve. With all this riding on the outcome, wouldn't you be more inclined to favor someone you know intimately with the prospect of helping you complete the project? Or are you willing to throw caution to the wind and ask the first stranger you encounter to help with such an important task after telling the person how much you favor him or her?

If you wanted to maximize the odds in your 'favor' you would most certainly ask someone with your 'favor' to do you a 'favor' so that the outcome would be the most favorable.

For anyone who may still have doubts about the blessed and favored status of human beings, the words Jesus spoke to a woman during one of his messages should make things much more clear,

> 'And it happened as He spoke these things, a certain woman of the company lifted up her voice and said to Him, Blessed is the womb that bore You, and the breasts which You have sucked. But He said, No; rather, blessed are they who hear the Word of God and keep it.'

Luke 11:27-28
Modern King James Version

Amazing! Here we witness Jesus preaching and performing miraculous signs and people are in various stages of awe, disbelief, and outright skepticism. Emotions are high when a woman from the crowd gets all worked-up and blurts out that the mother of Jesus is blessed from the womb to the bosoms, essentially confirming the angelic message given to Mary before Jesus was ever born.

Jesus had an opportunity at this very moment to affirm this excited woman's outburst and forever establish his mother's enviable position as the 'most-blessed' woman ever. But he did not!...at least he didn't leave the statement to stand alone, he added to it in a very meaningful and profound way.

Essentially Jesus said to the woman, "You're right! My mother is truly a blessed woman, I will not deny it. But those who hear and obey God's word are blessed, as well and I'd rather bless them. I choose to bless them over my own mother!" In one sentence Jesus lifts every person who hears and obeys his word to a higher level of blessing than even his own mother, who according to the God-sent angel Gabriel was 'blessed' above (all other) women.

The word 'rather' which Jesus used to describe the exact kind of blessing his followers would live in is translated from root words that mean 'very beautiful'. In effect, Jesus told this woman his followers-those who hear and obey his words,–would be *very beautifully* blessed far above the level of his own mother. What an awesome statement!

Jesus promotes and would rather bless people who hear and obey his words. The scriptures promise that people who believe in Jesus are seated with him in the heavenly places–high above every distraction, circumstance, predicament, whatever! You are blessed! You are *rather* blessed by the Spirit of God!

Certainly it should go almost without saying that the God of creation, who gave human beings the ultimate place of dominance on planet Earth, would want the very best for those created in His image and after His likeness. But the miracle is not that Jesus would say something so powerful and provocative, or even that God wants His children to be very beautifully blessed.

The most amazing miracle actually takes place when the children of God recognize, realize and accept the fact that God (the Father) wants to personally bless His children very beautifully, above and beyond current understanding and life circumstances….and then God's children begin to think, live, behave and speak like God wants to bless us very beautifully in every

41

aspect and part of our lives. That is precisely what Mary did and the rest is eternity.

The initial thought that God wants to bless people very beautifully is generally nice and easy to accept. We can even get on board with wishing that God would very beautifully bless others, especially those who live in abject poverty with absolutely no hope for life improvement, but we struggle with the concept that we can and should receive the very beautiful blessing of God personally for ourselves. Somehow when we imagine the very beautiful blessing of God being given to us directly and individually it loses its piety and holiness. The very beautiful blessing of God is something that should be bestowed upon someone else, but certainly we personally are just fine without it.

Thankfully, Mary did not suffer from such thoughts. But even if she did, in this instance she wisely kept quiet in front of Gabriel and allowed the God of Heaven to give her His very beautiful blessing, the privilege of giving birth to and raising the Son of God. We would all do well to imitate her humble silence and accept the abundant favor of God when He directs an opportunity for blessing our way.

Mary's Story: part III

So much had happened to Mary in such a short amount of time. She was trying her best just to make sense of it all. Only recently, her parents had introduced her to the carpenter Joseph and had arranged for her to be engaged to him. She was going to be married and so many questions were running through her head.

When had her parents met Joseph? How had Joseph even heard of her? When had her parents and Joseph started working on putting together a marriage proposal? What would the wedding be like? Who should she invite? What would she wear? Was Joseph's family excited for him? When would she meet them? Would Joe's family like her?

Mary was struggling to grasp onto what Gabriel had just told her about God's plan for her to bring the Messiah into the world. She did her best to try and remember what the angel had said to her. The baby God wanted her to give birth to would grow up and be great; the Son of the Highest. It was almost too much to imagine!

Although she was totally thankful she had been singled out by God for such an honor, she could not help but wonder, why her? Mary thought back to what her parents had been teaching her about prophecies concerning the coming of the Messiah. What was so special about this time in Israel right now? Why now?

Then something strange happened and a sense of fear invaded her mind. She was a VIRGIN! And she was engaged on top of that. What was Joseph going to say? What are my parents and friends going to think? How will I explain my growing tummy to the elders and leaders of the town? What will the priests think?

44

Mary needed a whole new set of answers to far more serious questions in light of what Gabriel had just dumped on her. Before he left, she needed to get some clarity and some peace for her chaos-filled mind. She knew the angel had to have the answers, especially if this was truly 'from God'. After all, God knows everything, doesn't He?

Mary mustered all her courage and looked at the angel straight in the eyes and let fly a question that would determine how everything from this moment on would work.

'Gabriel, Mary inquired, 'How can this be possible since I am a virgin?....

Chapter Three

Ask the Right Question

'Then Mary said to the angel, "How can this be, since I do not know a man?" And the angel answered and said to her, "The Holy Spirit will come upon you, and the power of the Highest will overshadow you; therefore, also, that Holy One who is to be born will be called the Son of God. "Now indeed, Elizabeth your relative *(cousin)** has also conceived a son in her old age; and this is now the sixth month for her who was called barren. "For with God nothing will be impossible."'

Luke 1:34-37
New King James Version
*parentheses and italics added

Mary accepted the favor of God on her life and the unique blessing of God wrapped within the unusual and very controversial task He was asking her to carry out for the eternal benefit of all mankind. The angel Gabriel had relayed God's request that Mary perform a favor for God by becoming pregnant with the only begotten Son of God, Jesus. Jesus is the Word of God made flesh through natural birth into the human plane of existence; God revealed in the flesh!

But Mary had a question for Gabriel, as any thinking girl most likely would in such a situation. The Bible records the question in such a way that in our modern era it is confused as something it is not. At first glance Mary's question seems pretty straight forward; how will she become pregnant without the involvement of a man. It seems as though Mary is fishing for a biological answer, but upon closer examination, Mary was asking about much more than just the birds and the bees.

Personally, I like how scripture phrases the beginning of her question; "How can this be…"? It is almost like she can't believe what the angel is saying to her is true, or that the event can even happen at all. We know that this is not the case, because the angel had been confronted earlier by another person who asked a very similar question when he was told his wife, Elizabeth, would have a child. And the angel's response was much, much different.

> 'There was in the days of Herod, the king of Judaea, a certain priest named Zacharias, of the course of Abia: and his wife was of the daughters of Aaron, and her name was Elisabeth. And they were both righteous before God, walking in all the commandments and ordinances of the Lord blameless. And they had no child, because that Elisabeth was barren, and they both were now well stricken in years. And it came to pass, that while he executed the priest's office before God in the order of his course, according to the custom of the priest's office, his lot was to burn incense when he went into the temple of the Lord. And there appeared unto him an angel of the Lord standing on the right side of the altar of incense. And when Zacharias saw him, he was troubled, and fear fell upon him. But

the angel said unto him, Fear not, Zacharias: for thy prayer is heard; and thy wife Elisabeth shall bear thee a son, and thou shalt call his name John. And Zacharias said unto the angel, Whereby shall I know this? for I am an old man, and my wife well stricken in years. And the angel answering said unto him, I am Gabriel, that stand in the presence of God; and am sent to speak unto thee, and to shew thee these glad tidings. And, behold, thou shalt be dumb, and not able to speak, until the day that these things shall be performed, because thou believest not my words, which shall be fulfilled in their season.'

Luke 1:5-13; 18-20

Zacharias was a priest and it was his privileged responsibility to light the incense at the temple. While he was carrying out this duty, an angel was sent by God to deliver some very good news for him and his wife, Elisabeth. They were going to have a child who would be the forerunner, or the one to announce the arrival of the Jewish Messiah.

Zach had an issue with the news however, and dared to ask the angel for clarifica-
tion. Zacharias' question; "Whereby shall I know
this?", or in other words or translations, "How
can I be sure of this? I am an old man and my
wife is well along in years." (Luke 1:18 NIV)

Certainly we should be able to understand
Zacharias' skepticism. He and Elisabeth had
most likely tried to have children throughout
their entire married lives together and now both
were well beyond child-bearing capabilities.
All Zach wanted was a clear understanding of
the details so he could be sure what the angel
said was true. What he was asking was not
that far removed from the question Mary would
ask some time later, "How can this be…?", but
the angel's response to Zacharias was much
harsher than his treatment of Mary.

Why did Zacharias receive such an apparently different and harsh response from God's
messenger?

Zacharias was in a sacred place as part of his
priestly responsibilities when the angel of the Lord
came to him with the news that he and his wife
Elisabeth were going to have a baby. As a priest
he should have been able to easily recognize a

50

spiritual, heavenly being such as an angel, and should have had the faith to believe whatever the message contained, as long as it conformed to the scriptures. There was absolutely no contradiction between what the angel said and the scriptures Zacharias would have known. In fact, there are many Old Testament instances where God intervened and helped barren women conceive children in cooperation with old or sterile husbands. Abraham and Sarah, the founding members of the Christian faith come quickly to mind, along with many others.

Zacharias was not so surprised by the visiting angel to the point where it is recorded that he freaked out. Yes, He was troubled and a little scared, but the angel assured him that good news was on the way. Zacharias even had a relaxed, civil conversation with the angel. He knew this angel was sent by God and he knew the angel's message was directly from God, yet Zacharias had the audacity to ask how he, an ordained representative of God for the people of Israel, could believe the message was true.

He basically told the angel to provide proof of the reality of God's message. Of course the angel provided it, but not in the manner

Zacharias expected. The angel's "proof" was a rebuke of Zach's unbelief. Simply put, Zach asked the wrong question to the right angel.

The angel told Zacharias that because he did not believe God's word he would be mute until the child was born and instead of naming the child Zach Jr., as was the tradition of the day, the child would be named John. Zacharias exited the sanctuary unable to talk. When the people gathered around him to find out what had taken so long in lighting the incense, he had to write down what had just occurred. Zacharias did not speak again until his son, John, was born.

Six months after visiting Zacharias, the angel was dispatched once again to the nation of Israel. But this time it was to Elizabeth's cousin, Mary. Mary listened to the message the angel related and then asked the angel one question; "How can this be...?"

This sounds eerily similar to the one Zacharias asked, but the angel responded very differently to her. The angel calmly, confidently explained to Mary how God would work things out. If Mary's question was the same as Zacharias', only expressed in a different way, then the angel was unjust in his 'punishment' of Zacharias and his kind treatment of Mary.

But Mary's question was not one that revealed perceived unbelief. Instead her question arose from a concern she inherently had for the success of God's plan. Mary lived in Israel, a nation where in times past prophets of God had foretold the arrival of the Messiah. Specifically, the prophet Isaiah declared,

> Therefore the Lord himself shall give you a sign; Behold, a virgin shall conceive, and bear a son, and shall call his name Immanuel.

Isaiah 7:14

Let's get some quick perspective on the situation Mary was facing with the proposal she received. Since many prophets had announced the coming messiah hundreds of years prior to Mary's existence, it was not a secret. Everyone in Israel was awaiting the arrival of the promised Messiah. Isaiah had done the other prophets one better by identifying the vehicle God would choose to bring the Messiah into the world, a virgin. Every Israelite with even a passing knowledge of the scriptures knew the Messiah would be born from a virgin.

The Law required that pregnant, single girls be punished by being stoned to death. Imagine a young girl living in a world where being pregnant without the benefit of a husband meant a very slow, painful death was only weeks or months away. Mary understood that she lived in a society that stoned pregnant virgins to death, so her question was not biological. It was totally practical and the angel answered appropriately.

In reality, Mary asked Gabriel how was she to live long enough after the telling baby bump became obvious, to carry this child from God to full term since she was a virgin. As soon as the leaders or elders of her town found out she was pregnant, they would judge her worthy of death. Gabriel assured her that the Holy Spirit would come over her and the power of the Highest would "overshadow" her, giving her the protection she needed not only to survive, but to successfully give birth to the One who would be known as Emmanuel-God with us!

It is imperative that when God asks us to do Him a favor, we ask the correct questions. In that moment, it is tempting to allow our humanity to

mess things up. Zacharias had become hard-
ened and cynical in his years of childlessness
with Elisabeth. When the angel Gabriel came
with good news of impending fatherhood, Zach
wanted proof. He did not care as to the details of
God's plan. He was not interested in helping God
succeed in sending someone who would pave
the way for Israel's true Messiah. He wanted a
tangible sign from God so he would know God
was really speaking through the angel. He got it,
but it was not what he expected or wanted.

Zacharias saw and had a conversation with
an angel! Does anyone really need proof after
such an encounter that what is said is true? No!
Zacharias revealed his self-interest and his lack
of faith by the question he posed. Mary, on the
other hand, revealed her humble desire to help
God with His redemptive plan by what she asked.

God has an amazing plan for each one of His
children. It most likely will not be on the scale of
a virgin birth, but it will be unique to the gifts God
has placed within each of His children. When
God reveals that plan, it is wise to remember
to ask the correct questions. Pose questions
which will give insight on just how God's plan
for your life can succeed. Ask how things can

get done, not just whether or not those things are true. God will always work with a person to ensure His plan will be accomplished. It is kind of funny to note that when God wants you, He will get His way, even if you don't believe Him. You just might be speechless for a while.

Mary did indeed see God's plan come to pass and God's highest power overshadowed her until she gave birth to Jesus. When Joseph, Mary's fiancé, found out she was pregnant, He could have publically denounced her as a trashy woman and lead the posse in stoning her to death. Instead, the Bible records that Joseph was a just man and did not want to humiliate Mary. He planned to cancel the wedding privately and let Mary deal with a baby he did not father. God sent an angel to counsel Joseph assuring him it was okay to take Mary as his bride because she was honorable and the baby was Divine.

God is always true to His word, even in unbelievable circumstances. Be like Mary and remember to ask the questions which will promote the success of God's plan and your particular involvement with it. We will explore the scope of God's overshadowing protection in a later chapter.

Mary's Story: Part IV

Mary didn't know exactly what to think of Gabriel's answer to her question. The Holy Spirit would come upon her. What did that mean? The power of the highest would overshadow her. Really? Mary didn't relish the idea of living under a cloud, even if it was "for God" like the angel promised!

Gabriel had seemed so reassuring while he was in her room and had answered the one and only question she heard herself blurt out. Why hadn't she asked more questions-like the ones flooding her mind at this precise moment? Mary was so conflicted. She didn't want to bother the angel, but he wasn't the one who had been asked to get pregnant, she was.

Gabriel was going on and on about something, but Mary had ceased being able to pay attention. The Holy Spirit, who is the Holy Spirit? She had never heard of such a person or anything like it. Mary had only gone to temple a few times in her life because it was so far away. And honestly, the journey was so tiring that by the time her family got to the court with everyone else all crowded around her, it was hard to make sense of what the priests were saying. She was sure that she had never heard them speak of a Holy Spirit before, though. Mary was curious.

She knew God is holy and she knew He didn't live on earth, so perhaps the angel was saying that God Himself would be on and in her life from now on. Her reasoning made sense, since Gabriel had said that the power of the Highest would be around too. Mary knew that there was no one more powerful than God. Calm was beginning to win the battle for her thoughts. She could hear herself breathing again.

Her thoughts came back to Gabriel. He was still there and he was talking about someone else now. He was saying something about her way older cousin, Elisabeth who was married to a priest in Jerusalem. Mary smiled when she thought of Elisabeth and her husband Zacharias. She had always liked them because they treated her like she was their child whenever her family went to visit. Mary wondered why Gabriel would be bringing up her cousin. Elisabeth couldn't have kids, everyone knew that.

Wait a minute, Mary thought, as the words Gabriel was speaking started to register. Elisabeth was pregnant! Could this be true? Zacharias and Elisabeth had tried to have kids for as long as Mary could remember, but here was an angel telling her that Elisabeth was six months along! Mary was astonished, shocked and completely relieved all at once. As Gabriel was speaking the words, "For with God nothing shall be impossible", she was thinking almost the same thing.

Mary was thinking that even though she loved Elisabeth, Elisabeth and Zacharias were really old: beyond having babies old. If God could do the impossible for Elisabeth, Mary knew in that moment that God could and would do the impossible for her. Mary didn't know all the details, but she knew that the Holy Spirit was going to come upon her and the power of the Highest would cover her and that was all she needed to know.

"Thank-you God for Zacharias and Elisabeth", Mary thought. I needed to hear some good news before I gave Gabriel my answer to your proposal....

Chapter Four

Take Encouragement from What God is doing for Others Now

"And, behold, thy cousin Elisabeth, she hath also conceived a son in her old age: and this is the sixth month with her, who was called barren. For with God nothing shall be impossible."

Luke 1:36-37

Mary just got hit with the news of a lifetime. She was being asked to carry the Messiah, God in the flesh, the Redeemer of all mankind, the King of kings in her womb for nine months, give birth to and raise the Son of God. WOW!! Talk about too much.

When God opens up an opportunity for you to reveal His awesomeness, it will seem too good to be true. After all, who are you that God should show off through you? I'm sure Mary was thinking along those lines when Gabriel added those powerful words of encouragement to his address. The gist of what he said was God did something wonderful for your relative just the other day, so take heart, He can do something wonderful for you today.

Whether we are being faced with the God opportunity of a lifetime or we are facing our darkest day of challenge, Christians need to learn to get encouragement from others who have faced, or are facing similar circumstances. Gabriel knew Mary would need a strong boost of God confidence, so he told her something currently happening in the life of a close family member with which she could easily relate.

I love the fact that Gabriel did not wax religious with Mary and clear his throat, get a deep and pious tone and say, "Remembereth thou the God of Abraham, Isaac and Jacob. What thy God hath performed thousands of years ago, that which hath no bearing upon your life today, God wilt doeth again. Be at peace, girl"! Said no angel, ever! No! Gabriel utilized a relevant, present day situation involving someone Mary knew personally to highlight God's ability to perform what He promised to Mary.

The good news Gabriel shared with Mary needs to serve as an example for us today. We all need encouragement from time to time and it is nice to get that encouragement from friendly sources familiar with God's amazing power. Even though God has promised that He has the best of intentions for us, ala Jeremiah 29:11–and He does have great plans for His children–sometimes the physical part of living them out, gets heavy. We all have our fair share of good and bad experiences.

Many times we get frustrated and depressed when blessings occur or challenges arise. The dominant culture of 'correctness' in which we live today causes us to be hyper sensitive as though it is impolite or selfish or even outright bragging to tell someone else about our blessing-me included. When something good happens to us or we receive a blessing, it is easy to think we might come across as merely attention seeking, über-righteous snobs if we share the news with anyone but our closest friends. And really just who are we anyway to receive such good fortune?

If we are going through a hard time or difficult circumstances, we may feel as though we are

all alone-the only person going through whatever it is we're facing; others won't understand,
or we'll be scolded as whining and wanting pity.
So we suffer silently and make things worse by
trying to 'be strong in the Lord and in the power
of His might', when a faith-filled friend may be
waiting to help us with timely support.

One final thought on this topic; we need to
guard our hearts and thoughts against being
jealous of someone else's success, even when
it is someone we don't especially like or think
deserved the dream-come-true moment we
witness the person enjoying. When we look at
another person's story, it is not so we become
negative, jealous or bitter. Our God wants the
very best for all humanity. The Bible is clear that
God sends the rain for the just and the unjust.
We need to be happy for people who are living
in a moment of God-given victory.

The key to remaining upbeat and on task
for God is to find current, relevant stories about
people, locally or globally, and draw encouragement from shared, in-common experiences. Mary
drew strength from learning about Elisabeth.
For both these ladies, this was a high day for
celebrating God's goodness. Mary kept drawing

strength and encouragement from others all the way to the cross on which her son was nailed. In that horrific moment, she was comforted by Mary Magdalene and her son, John.

Years later, when the apostle Paul wrote letters to the churches he had established, he encouraged the people in those churches to trust in God's faithfulness through hard times, because God had been faithful to him during imprisonments, beatings and even being left for dead. Paul didn't go to a religious galaxy far, far away for examples; he used his nasty nows as illustrations to benefit the members of the growing church and to rally Believers around God's overall plan for eternal victory.

Even when God shows us exactly what He has for us, as He did for Mary, it can be borderline too much. He is the God that can do exceeding, abundantly above all that we can ask or think, after all. And that is when His power is already at work in us! We get overwhelmed with the sheer magnitude of what God is asking us to perform and we may think, "No way, I'm just,…I can't,…someone else should,…."

That is the precise moment we need to find a current, real-time example of someone who God is assisting in the same kind of way and remind ourselves that what God does for one, He will do for another. In the times we live in there is no shortage of great God-stories to boost our belief in God's goodness and faithfulness.

How many dreams have people, Christians and non-Christians alike, forfeited because of the seeming impossibility and bigness of the idea or desire? And how many dreams have people forfeited because of frustration and disillusionment at the success of some other person, whose life appears easier than seems fair; God must have liked them better. Your God loves the world and those in it equally. He has a plan for those who love Him and it will come to pass at the right time as believers remain faithful to God, in good times as well as bad times.

Remember to take strength and encouragement from your contemporaries, those people who are going through some of the same things you are working through. If God is blessing them, if those you are watching, and perhaps even serving can make it, then God will bless you and you can make it through, too.

Mary's Story: Part V

Mary was still in a state of shock at Gabriel's news about her cousin Elisabeth being pregnant. How cool was that! It was just the news she needed to hear to kind of make sense of everything else that was happening around and to her. Elisabeth and Zacharias were going to have a baby! How many times had Mary herself prayed for Elisabeth and Zacharias to have a wonderful, little bundle of joy? God really could do the impossible.

For some reason she could not quite understand, Elisabeth being pregnant gave her a confidence that had been absent before. If God could watch over an old, barren woman to ensure that she and her baby would both be safe, then God could surely watch over Mary and keep her safe from the people who would not understand or believe her story. She wasn't even worried about what Joseph might think.

That little tidbit was pretty amazing in itself, because over the time of her engagement, she had become more and more enamored with her handsome carpenter. Right now Joseph was preparing a new home as a present to her for the wedding night and beyond. If Joseph found out she was pregnant, what would he say? What would he do? Mary didn't know, and at that moment, didn't care. With God nothing shall be impossible was all she could think about. And Elisabeth was living proof of that fact.

With God, nothing shall be impossible. Mary was interested in seeing just exactly what, with God, was possible.

"Gabriel," Mary started, "you've convinced me. I'll do it, just like you said."

Chapter Five

Seize the Opportunity

'Then Mary said, "Behold the
maidservant of the Lord! Let it be
to me according to your word."
And the angel departed from her.'

Luke 1:38
New King James Version

Mary said yes! She said better than yes.
Mary told Gabriel that she wanted what
he had told her was going to happen to move
forward exactly as he had stated. She didn't
negotiate for advantage, position or fame. She
said, I'm yours, do what you will, according to
what you said.

Oftentimes opportunity knocks on the door
of our lives and we don't answer. We know that

God has an awesome plan for us, but when it shows up, it is not quite what we imagined, or it might cost us more than we thought it was going to. We ignore the God-moment and he moves on, leaving us wondering why adventure eludes our lives and blaming Him for not using us.

Mary could have said no to the angel. She might have even given very serious thought to telling the angel to go pound sand, but bottom line, she didn't. Mary leaped at the chance to do something wonderful for God, which in turn would impact the entire world—forever. The rest, we might say, is history,…or herstory, if we want to be cute. But let's examine what Mary said 'yes' to.

Mary was a single woman in a small town.
　She risked getting a bad reputation.
Mary was engaged to a man who owned a business and had position.
　She risked being rejected and publically humiliated.
Mary lived in a place and time that condemned 'loose women' to death.
　She risked false accusation and death.

Mary received no guarantees that God would do any more for her than make sure the baby was delivered in nine months.

She risked death, hardship, living in poverty, single-parenthood and having her child be known for life as illegitimate.

Clearly what Mary was presented with was not exactly the blessed opportunity most modern Christians would eagerly embrace, even with an angelic invitation. But Mary said yes!

We live in a theological time where it seems that all we read, hear and see is how much God wants us to be blessed, prosperous, pain-free and living large. Please understand, I believe God is a God of prosperity and wants His children to be blessed. But not for the sake of being blessed; Christians are blessed,….<get this>…. to be a blessing!

Mary said yes to a plan that carried no personal guarantees. She risked everything so that she could bring into the world, how did Gabriel put it,

> "He will be great, and will be called the Son of the Highest; and the Lord God will give Him the throne

of His father David. "And He will
reign over the house of Jacob forever, and of His kingdom there will
be no end."

Luke 1:32-33
New King James Version

There is not one thing in what Gabriel said
that remotely references Mary will even be
remembered as the child's mother, but she said
yes. Many times in our 21st century spirituality we
want the blessing of God just so we can simply
prove to our peers how spiritual and accepted
by God we think others should know we are. We
live in a pseudo-Christian competition which mir-
rors the world's mantra, "The guy with the most
toys wins", except ours is "The most blessed
Believer is the most closest to God".

In the Christian world not so long ago,
when something bad happened to a Christian;
physical, financial, emotional, whatever, other
Christians would distance themselves from the
person, because associating with any hardship
might rub off. The always unasked question was,
"What did you do to make God mad?" Before I
get into too much trouble, with an audience I'm

trying to persuade, answer this question. How many Christians do you know that would invite a young girl from church into their homes after it was revealed she had become pregnant outside of being married?

Thankfully, the hyper-religious atmosphere that once dominated Christian culture has cleared and for the most part Christians today show the love and compassion Jesus show-cased and boldly stated would be the manner for others to know we are His followers. But think about the time in which Mary lived and ask how many people would have invited Mary to come for an extended stay, especially after her belly began to grow?

Mary said yes to God after He offered her rejection, pain, humiliation, potential poverty and maybe even death. Wait a minute, I meant to say she said yes to carrying the savior of the world; what a blessing. Mary's thoughts were not on herself, or she would have said no. Instead her thoughts were on blessing humanity for all time and she said yes.

God's opportunities for us to do great things rarely come with up front celebrity, acceptance, wealth or security. God asks His children to take a great risk, for a great reward. We like to quote John 3:16 to showcase God's love for the world. But when God risked His only son, there were no guarantees that anyone would respond favorably to such a sacrificial display of love. In fact, the apostle Paul would later pen that while we were still sinners, actively rejecting God, He sent His son to redeem us. Only in great risk, can great reward be obtained.

Today, we need to reexamine what we suppose a God opportunity looks like and rethink our responses to the ones we may have missed. God may ask you to do something for Him that at first glance may look to others like you blew it; think out-of-wedlock pregnancy. How many people tsk'ed, tsk'ed Mary and shook their heads or pointed fingers at the poor girl who had made such a horrible mistake? Oh, you mean the mistake of giving the world a redeemer? Yee-ha!

What will you say yes to? Or maybe the question should be, what will you stop, breathe, and think about before just saying no, and what will you work through the possibilities of what might be in the future, if you can suffer through a little present pain? God has a plan for you. Say yes.

Mary's Story: part VI

Mary had said yes to God's plan for her to bring the long-awaited Messiah into the world. The reality of her decision had not quite sunk in and really she didn't want to think too hard on the consequences which were sure to come. In mere months, people would not be able to help but notice a nicely shaped baby bump rising from her mid-section.

What was she going to do? Where's the angel when you really need him? Nice, that—deliver a message, then leave. No advice, no plan of action, no possible explanations, just,....POOF!,... gone. Great! Now what? Mary thought for a few seconds about what options she had immediately available to her. She quickly concluded, not so many. Mary started to freak out.

Then, in just moments, a peaceful calm enveloped her and she breathed in slowly. She breathed out. She wondered what her cousin Elisabeth was going through. Six months along the angel had told her. ELISABETH, Mary thought! Of course! Here was Mary all freaking out about what was going to happen to her and Elisabeth was heading into the final months of her pregnancy without the assistance of a close relative.

Mary raced to pack her clothes. She was going to pay a visit to her old cousin Elisabeth and see if she might be able to help her and Zacharias until the new baby arrived. Mary scoured her closet and quickly stuffed a suitcase full of things she would need for a long-term visit to Jerusalem. Oh, why hadn't Elisabeth told her sooner that she was preggers? How exciting this was all going to be. Mary's heart was racing as she left a quick note so her parents wouldn't worry and left her home, closing the door behind her.

Mary smiled. Her adventure had begun...

Chapter Six

Go on Vacation

Really, when God gives you a plan and you agree to work it through for Him, it will most likely be bigger and grander than you can imagine or figure out. If you think too much, you will probably stress yourself out, or go crazy, so you might just as well relax and take a trip away from the circumstance.

> 'Now Mary arose in those days and went into the hill country with haste, to a city of Judah, and entered the house of Zacharias and greeted Elizabeth.'

Luke 1:39-40
New King James Version

Mary could have stayed in her hometown. It would have been convenient and familiar, but it would have been tense, as well. Mary would be constantly looking over her shoulder, because certainly in the coming days, people would begin to wonder and question what exactly was going on with the young lady's tummy.

But God had promised Mary that the child would be born in His message from Gabriel. A worst case scenario would be that Mary would have to be whisked out of town by some spiritual beings to the amazement of the crowds coming to kill her. It would create some really good buzz for the tabloids, but God had a better idea.

Mary immediately packed her stuff and went to a place where not so many people knew her. In essence she went on vacation. Now before we get this romantic image of a young pregnant woman sitting poolside sipping virgin daiquiri's, remember she would be killed, if anyone found out she was with child.

But the principle is still valid. When you are working God's plan, it is best to allow Him the freedom to ensure the plan's success. A lot of times we derail God's best efforts through trying to help Him with the details. We think He is moving too slow, or is using the wrong people to help us with what is essentially our destiny, so we extend a helping hand to God and mess things up.

It is usually best to leave the workings of God's plan to God and do only what He has asked us to do in our part of His plan. Many a Sunday school story revolves around people in the Bible who blew it by doing more or by doing less than what God had for them to do. Mary's job was to incubate a baby, no more, no less. So she wisely went to Elisabeth's house and got busy doing something else to take her mind off the baby growing in her womb. Mary still had to be on guard, though.

If you think Mary made it easy on God by leaving town, you need to think again. Mary went to the bustling city of Jerusalem, the epi-center of temple worship. Every priest, every pious person, everyone who even had a passing thought about God would be in that city, looking for ways to bring the righteousness of God to a public forum. Virginal, pregnant Mary went right into the middle of the most religious city on the planet to live with her priest cousin-in-law, who had created quite the stir by being struck mute while lighting incense in the temple.

And if that weren't enough, the woman he was married to, who everyone knew had been barren, was now six months along in her own pregnancy. Of course married people having kids is just run of the mill normal, but this couple was old, too old to have kids. Move along, nothing to see here, yeah, right! Imagine the publicity that surrounded Zacharias and Elisabeth.

Everyday people would want to know if Zach could talk yet and all the women who even vaguely knew Elisabeth would be ooh-ing and cooing over her ever increasing in size belly. Zacharias and Elisabeth would have been front page news on every paper in town and the blogosphere would be on fire with status updates, likes and tweets about the soon to be born baby.

Mary could not have picked a more stressful place to relax and hide if she had tried. But God is so good, He knew the best place to hide a pregnant girl was in a place with so many other differing and similar distractions, Mary would be safely invisible. She would indeed be able to relax and give the growing baby Jesus a restful time of in vitro bliss during the most important time of His physical formation.

We need to take note of this unusual, yet wise move Mary made concerning her mental, emotional, physical and spiritual well-being. She didn't hide away at home, wondering when the pregnancy police would find her. Mary didn't try to come up with radical rescue plans in the event she was discovered. Mary went on vacation to a place where only God's overshadowing power could hide her.

When we are released to bring God's plan for our lives into the earth, it is best for us to remember to stay humble. We did not formulate or initiate the plan and the best we can do by trying to help is slow it down, so we need to relax and let God do what He does best; bring Glory to Himself through us. Somehow, Mary knew innately that if she stayed at home, it would not be optimal. The tension and pressure of every day seeing and interacting with people who knew her intimately would be too much. We could question the wisdom of where she ultimately went, but it seems to have worked out fine two-thousand odd years later.

Mary's move teaches us that God wants us at ease while we are carrying out His plan. Jesus told His disciples that His yoke was easy and His burden light, so why do we stress when God gives us a task to carry out? If He told us to do something, it is up to Him to give us the power to do it. God will make a way when we get out of the way.

Please understand, I am not suggesting that we should physically move from one town to another, like Mary. I am strongly recommending that we relax, take our hands off the issues at hand and just let God handle the situations as only He can. It is ultra-important that we let His Holy Spirit live in us and let His highest power overshadow us, as we faithfully obey what He has asked us to do. No more, no less. Mary's vacation involved visiting her cousin in Jerusalem. Your 'vacation' may require that you find a good book to read, or go to your favorite hangout. Whatever it is just remember to relax and have a good time while God does what only He can.

You stressing will not make God's plan move any faster than He wants it to and you'll be miserable and prone to goofing things up. Vacations are much more profitable for you. Bye now, send a postcard.

Mary's Story: part VII

Mary could not believe the size of Elisabeth's belly!

"You're only six months along?" she asked as she placed both hands on Elisabeth's roundly protruding belly. "There's so something about your God"!

"My God?", Elisabeth countered, "He's your God, too!"

"I know, I know, but this is your moment. I don't even look pregnant, but you, you are totally huge." Mary laughed. "I am so happy for you, Elisabeth! Thank-you for letting me come stay with you for awhile."

"Zacharias and I are happy to have you, although he won't say so, Elisabeth paused momentarily, "...at least not until after the baby comes."

Mary and Elisabeth both laughed so hard at the joke they had tears streaming down their faces. Mary was glad to see her cousin in such high spirits. She later excused herself and settled into her new surroundings.

If she were to be totally honest with herself, this brief time alone was really the only time she had really reflected on the recent events in her life. Her life was about to get beyond crazy. Soon Joseph would find out where she had disappeared to and who knew what he would do then. Mary's parents could put off the inevitable for only so long.

Zacharias and Elisabeth would be welcoming a new addition to a long-established two-person family and all the friends and other relatives who had never believed or even dreamed children were a possibility for Zacharias and Elisabeth would be swarming all over the place she now temporarily called home. In spite of the attention her newest, tiny relative would receive, Mary knew there would be a lot of very uncomfortable questions pointed in her direction; ones she was unsure of how to answer, without giving away her secret.

There was a collision coming very soon unless God did something radically amazing. But what, she wondered, could he do? In her haste to come to Jerusalem to see Elisabeth, it had not dawned on her that this house was a center of attention. She was going to get found out, caught, and then...she shuddered. Even Elisabeth's unborn baby had sensed something was up, according to Elisabeth's telling.

When Mary had first come into the house, Elisabeth had screamed. Mary thought it was simply from Elisabeth's surprise at seeing her, but then she told Mary that the baby had leaped for joy at seeing her because of the 'package' she carried. How had she thought coming to Elisabeth's home was a good idea?

Mary sat down on the bed, exhausted from her trip and from thinking too hard over her circumstances. She closed her eyes and sighed. She could do nothing about what was headed her way, so she surrendered to the unknown.

Instantly a song entered her mind and she began to sing out loud, "My soul does magnify the LORD and my spirit has rejoiced in God, my Savior. For He that is mighty has done great things, and holy is His name. In that split-second moment, Mary could feel what the angel Gabriel had promised. The overshadowing presence of the Holy Spirit engulfed her and such a peace invaded every nook and cranny of her worry-dimpled mind.

Before Mary drifted off into a deep, refreshing sleep, she determined that from now on until this adventure was over, she was going to make her God bigger and bigger in her life; body, soul and spirit. Mary was going to magnify and make her God bigger, forever!

Chapter Seven

Make Your God Bigger

'And Mary said, My soul doth magnify the Lord, And my spirit hath
rejoiced in God my Saviour. For
he hath regarded the low estate
of his handmaiden: for, behold,
from henceforth all generations
shall call me blessed. For he that
is mighty hath done to me great
things; and holy is his name.'

Luke 1:46-49

The young, single, woman, Mary, a virgin, has said 'yes' to God's plan which requires her to become pregnant with the Son of God. Mary has decided that her best option is to visit her cousin, Elisabeth in Jerusalem for a few months. To be sure, their home is a hotbed of attention and activity.

Both Zacharias and Elisabeth were "well-stricken" with age, according to the Bible, so it is understandable that Zach would be some-what skeptical about what the angel said. An old, highly publically made mute priest and his equally as old wife, whose well-known repu-tation was that she could not have kids, were about to have a baby. That is news, anytime, anywhere. Hello, Mary, welcome to mayhem!

But the something about Mary, which most likely set her apart from other maidens of her day, was her ability to recognize the need for an ever-getting-bigger God constantly and consistently at work in her life. As soon as she and Elisabeth finished exchanging greetings and pleasantries, Mary began to magnify God in a praise. Mary went on praising her God and expounding about Him for nine verses! Remember that this entire study is taken from a sum total of thirty verses. For almost one-third of this particular time God is being made bigger and bigger by Mary. Nine verses!

God is sometimes lucky to get nine words from us as we get lost in the trappings of our post-modern era. It is so fitting that this initial episode in Mary's pregnancy ends with her magnifying God. She displays a powerful principle at the outset of what will be a very trying time in her life; she makes God bigger! Mary enlarges God in her life.

Take special note of this fact. Mary was at a high point in her timeline of carrying God's child. No one besides Mary and Elisabeth (and Elisabeth's still-in-the- womb baby), are known to have been in on Mary's secret. She wasn't showing. She wasn't to the point of having morning sickness, swellings or cravings. Joseph still loved her and intended to marry her. And her cousin, who could not have kids, was pregnant and had opened her home to Mary for a prolonged visit. Life was very good at that particular moment.

So what did Mary do? Sit back and relax? Eat bon-bons and pickles? Wait to include God, until crises and panic overwhelmed her? No, on all counts,…well, maybe, but for sure a resounding 'no' on the last one. Mary understood that the only way she was going to be successful in her life, carrying and raising this Holy child, was for her to make God the biggest focal point in everything she undertook. And there was no time to waste, or no time like the present, to begin making God bigger, which she did.

By magnifying God, purposefully making Him exponentially larger and larger in her life, Mary forfeited many of the battles she would have to face in the coming months over to the God who was more able to win them for her anyway. Think about just this one aspect of Mary's situation; Joseph. Mary needed to say something to her fiancé. She hadn't even bothered to consult him before giving the angel her affirmative answer to becoming pregnant in the first place. Make God bigger!

Mary could have easily stressed out about what she might say to her future husband to the point of making herself sick. Realistically, there was nothing she could do to explain to Joseph in any believable way that she had become pregnant by the Holy Spirit. Make God bigger, let Him deal with Joseph. Joseph was going to put Mary away, albeit privately, but her fiancé was outta there. Gabriel shows up and in divine fashion, only a short dream later, Joseph is as 'on board' with the plan as Mary's baby. Make God bigger!

God had to intervene on Mary's behalf so many times and in so many diverse ways that if Mary had decided to be a grown-up and handle all the issues herself, we would still be waiting for salvation today. If the pious crowds had not killed her, the stress and complicated logistics of bringing the Christ-child into the world by herself would have. Make God bigger!

But Mary lived in a simpler time, you might say. Technology and fast-paced lifestyles make it more difficult and less convenient to make God larger in our lives today. Those two modern advancements alone make it all the more necessary for Christians today to stop and purposely, consciously increase the size of the most majestic God and His involvement in regular, daily life. If Mary needed a bigger God in simpler times just to survive her pregnancy, how much bigger, larger, more important and more magnificent should we make and allow our God to be in us today? Make your God bigger!

Magnify God in your life today, this instant. Then purpose to make Him even more integral tomorrow, bigger than He is today. The author of the book of Hebrews made a point to say that Jesus Christ is the same yesterday, today and forever. Let God be the same in your life–always getting more and more relevant, more and more important, ever increasing in magnification–yesterday, today, tomorrow, the day after tomorrow and forever.

Mary did it. Things worked out okay for her. Make...your...God...**BIGGER!**

Mary's Story: part VIII

Mary was devastated! She could not control her sobs. There were others around her, crying with her, trying to console her, but she was blind and numb to the clumsy, but heart-felt efforts. Her baby boy, her first-born son was slowly dying in agony!

Her mind raced back to that glorious day so many years ago when Gabriel had appeared to her and announced that she would bring the Messiah into the world, if she agreed to God's plan. What were the words he used to describe her Jesus,

He shall be great, and shall be called the Son of the Highest: and the Lord God shall give unto him the throne of his father David: and he shall reign over the house of Jacob forever and of his kingdom there shall be no end.[1]

What on earth,...NO! what in ~~Heaven's~~ name had occurred in the years since Gabriel's amazing visit that she would now be watching her son hang on Rome's worst horror, a cross for criminals? Her son was not a criminal! He was the Son of God! Even in the confusion at what she was witnessing, Mary was more convinced of that fact than at any time before.

A small laugh invaded her sorrow as a long-forgotten memory resurfaced. How frantically she and Joseph had searched for Jesus all over the city of Jerusalem. Jesus had only been twelve at the time and Mary was mortified that she had lost the Son of God. "We just didn't know he was gone."

She saw herself before God's throne trying to explain how she had doomed humanity through one minute of careless assumption. Both she and Joseph were clueless as to how Jesus had managed

_____

1   Luke 1:32, 33

to elude the entire family's pilgrimage for three days as they were heading home from temple worship. "I thought He was with other family members." Mary had wondered at the time, if God would find her explanation worthy of forgiving, or if she had stretched the envelope of God's mercy just a bit too far this time.

When Mary and Joseph finally found Him at the temple, Jesus seemed so calm and relaxed among the religious leaders he was talking with. Mary was equal parts angry, relieved, amazed and proud of her son. And the Elders were astonished at His knowledge of the scriptures. She remembered thinking to herself at the time, "Well He is the Word of God in the flesh." It looked like Joseph wanted to kill him when Jesus flatly stated that it was time for him to be about his father's business. Neither Joseph nor Mary had really understood what Jesus was saying, they just thought he was being sassy. Oh, to live those days again, Mary thought, as sobs overtook her once more.

Jesus looked down from the hideous death perch he had been nailed upon and quietly said something to her, then to another one of her sons, John who knelt beside her. ~~Afterward~~ Jesus was silent, but very quickly, Mary felt John's strong arm around her and she knew that she would be taken care of by him from that time on. Jesus loved his half-brother John, who was also a devoted follower of his older brother. Mary was relieved that she would be welcome in John's home.

It seemed like an eternity had passed before she was startled out of her grief by a loud yell. It was Jesus and he was screaming something. His pained, mournful voice pierced her heart and she involuntarily put her hands to her ears to block out sounds of her son ready to die. Mary heard Jesus ask his father why he had been left alone, abandoned to die. "Into your hands I give my spirit," Jesus heaved a final breath and Mary watched his body go limp. Mary convulsed with tears and grief; her son, who would be king forever, was dead. God's dream for humanity's redemption would not come true now.

Mary was lost once more in her memories of living with Jesus. She remembered his hesitancy at turning water into wine. She was so furious with him at the time because he dared talk back to his own mother, and at a wedding of all places. She angrily told the wine stewards to, "do whatever he tells you to do", and then went to Jesus and told him to obey his mother. Everyone at the wedding agreed it was the best-tasting wine, ever.

She thought back to the time when she temporarily lost faith that Jesus was really the Son of God, regardless of what Gabriel had said. Jesus had been just plain acting weird; preaching in the homes of stranger's, healing all kinds of sick folk and telling demons and devils to leave other people. He certainly had not been acting kingly or messiah-ish, in her mind. So she had rallied the kids together and the family was going to have an intervention. Mary had grown tired of people spreading rumors about her son.

Mary and some of her children all went to a house where Jesus was holding meetings and tried to get him to come out so he could be taken to for professional evaluation. Jesus snubbed them all-then had the audacity to ask the group listening to him who his mother and siblings were. Mary was incredulous and embarrassed. It was completely obvious to everyone that Jesus' family was just outside. To bring a head to all the awkwardness, some people had torn the roof off the place and had lowered down a sick friend so Jesus could heal him. People were definitely going to talk,...a lot. And they did.

Mary's small relief was brought to a very gory conclusion when she heard a gasp from one of the people in her group. She looked up just in time to see a Roman soldier brutally stab her Jesus in the side with a long spear. Was there no end to the barbarism the Romans could display? Jesus was obviously very dead as any passing glance would prove, yet these guys had to be sure.

With all that had been done to torture Jesus in the last 24-hours, stabbing him just seemed like killing him twice. Mary was about to say something out of character, when she heard the soldier holding the spear whisper something that would remain in her mind until the day she died. "This man was truly the Son of God". The soldier's tone was a mixture of extreme fear and holy reverence. Mary cried.

Mary was lost in a grief-stricken trance for the next few days. She knew there were people around her trying to comfort her and to help her personally come to grips with what had been done to Jesus, but it was so easy to just ignore everything and everybody. Hopefully the friends and followers of her son would disperse soon and leave her to a quiet, lonely and sad existence. Mary could not figure out why God would allow His only Son to die and die in such a cruel manner. She was really struggling with trying to understand what God was thinking or planning now.

A young woman named Mary Magdalene interrupted her painful reflections. It was the first day of the week and a group of ladies had planned to go put oils and spices on the body of Jesus so he wouldn't stink. It would be the first opportunity to do anything 'nice' for him, since Jesus had been killed on the eve of the Sabbath and by law no one could touch him during this time of reverent worship. Mary quietly prepared the perfumes that she had chosen to pour over her son. Her pain was indescribable; her angel-announced, God-induced, Spirit-protected son was dead. DEAD! And all she had was a few fading memories of someone wonderful.

She would accompany her friends to the tomb where Jesus had been buried, but she was not sure how she would react when she got there. And who would roll the stone away for them? Mary could not count on the men who had followed Jesus for the last three years to be of any help. The disciples had all disappeared after Jesus had been arrested in the garden. Jesus had just been finishing up his prayers when the soldiers attacked him and took him to trial...at midnight. Mary did not want to relive that hideous night, so she refocused her efforts on preparing her potions.

A little while later the women left together for the tomb. Thankfully, it was not a long walk, so Mary would not get too absorbed in reminiscing about Jesus. Mary's thoughts returned to the group when she heard them murmuring that they were getting close. Her heart began to pound and it was more difficult to breathe. She looked up and to her amazement the tomb was already open.

There was a strange, but at the same time familiar-looking man sitting on what appeared to be the stone that had been placed on the door. As the women all ran to find out what was going on, questions were forming in Mary's mind. Questions that man sitting so smugly on the slab of rock in front of her son's tomb had better be prepared to answer, or else.

As Mary got close, she heard the man say something wonderfully familiar, "Don't be afraid." Every memory of every bad thing that had happened in the past few days evaporated as those words registered in her spirit. The next time the unearthly being spoke, sweet clarity consumed her and everything Jesus had said to Mary over their years as family, mother and son, finally and eternally made sense.

"He is not here, He is risen..."

Chapter Eight

Begin Your Adventure

Mary's story is a wonderful adventure. If we were pressed to describe her life today, it would be safe to say Mary's was a roller-coaster ride on an epic scale. She lived faithful to the call God placed upon her life and even overcame personal doubts and questions to arrive at a genuine faith in Jesus, as her redeemer. Christians in the modern or post-modern era would do well in learning from her principled example.

In her day, Mary didn't have the resources available to her that we so casually take for granted today, but she romped it-spiritually speaking. All she had was an abiding trust in the God she knew and she believed He would win out over any situation or circumstance she faced.

She believed she was favored and that she lived in a favored environment. Mary didn't try to dismiss the favor, she accepted it as part of God's overarching plan for her life. Years later when a woman who basically had no clue, tried to pronounce a blessing over Mary, Jesus himself said that those who obey God now are more blessed than Mary. It would be rude not to mention that we are more blessed, because Mary was blessed, but the point is,...we are MORE blessed. Accept it and live it. Quit whining for it. Humility is simply living in God's favor, while doing God a favor.

Mary displayed an eagerness to understand God's plan. She did not waste time wondering if it was true, she just wanted to know how God was going to pull it off so she wouldn't slow it down or screw it up. When we believe God is true in whatever He says, it will help us to formulate the right questions to ask to maximize our cooperative success. Remember we are working with Him, as well as for Him. Asking the right questions reveals your faith in the truthfulness of God's word. He is always pleased when His kids believe Him.

It is hard to believe God sometimes. Life throws unexpected curves at us from time to time. Prayers seem to go unanswered and bad things happen to good people. And frankly, sometimes Bible stories read like fairytales. The miracles it records happened so long ago, it's hard to believe them today. Don't let life, and the living of it, discourage you. God is moving and doing great things in people all around. People you know.

Gabriel knew it would be hard for Mary to believe his announcement if he came to her talking about Sarah, or Rachel, or Hannah, even though each woman had been blessed with a miracle baby at one time. They were godly women, to be sure, but their times of life were so far removed from when and where Mary was living, it would have been very difficult for her to relate to their success stories.

Mary knew Elisabeth personally. Mary and Elisabeth were cousins and Mary knew Elisabeth could not have kids, ever. When Gabriel told Mary that Elisabeth was six months into being pregnant, it was just the right thing to say in order to boost Mary's faith enabling her to believe God could do what the angel was promising.

Find where God is doing awesome, miraculous things in and for people today, in a time-frame that makes sense to you right now, not ten, five, two-thousand plus years ago. The true stories in the Bible are there to prove that nothing is impossible with God. What He is doing in and for His people today proves that He was, is, and will forever be the same; always awesome and amazing.

If you are sick, find someone whom God has healed and listen with focused attention to what God has performed for him or her. Have that person who is living and showing off God's personal healing power pray for you; God will heal you, too. If you need financial breakthrough, find someone for whom God has just provided finances and ask them to pray with you. Whatever you need to believe, God has probably done it for someone not too far removed from you in the last year, month, week, day, hour, or minute. Find them and take heart and encouragement from the experience happening to them, right in this contemporary moment. Mary did, so what's the problem with you?

Say yes to God. Better yet, ALWAYS say yes to God. Seize the God-moment! Even when our feelings of inadequacy might want to stop us, saying yes to God is always good for us in the long run. Mary said yes without knowing every minute detail of how saying yes would affect and impact her life. She just said yes. In the decade of the eighties, there was an anti-drug campaign spear-headed by America's First Lady Nancy Reagan. The slogan was, "Just say NO!" Unfortunately, that mind-set has infiltrated the church many times in the decades since. I have succumbed to it myself more times than I would care to admit.

It is time for a church-wide movement of "Just say YES!" Say yes to God, say yes to adventure, say yes to the unknown, say yes to bigger things than you've imagined. Say Yes! Say yes until God hears you, say it so loudly He can't ignore you or tune you out. Mary said yes. We should too!

Once 'yes' has been achieved, learn to relax and let God do what only God can do; namely the impossible. A virginal Mary, who tried to help God out by getting pregnant, would not have remained virginal for very long and would have only disqualified herself from God's plan…by trying to help. Many years ago, my wife and I lived in Texas. While there we met a completely cool man that was fond of telling us what people said in Texas. He would say, "We have a saying here in Texas…", and then expound some Texas-sized wisdom. One of the things he was quick to tell us originated in Texas was, "If you have to tell someone you're helping them, you're not".

In truth and actuality, I think God initially coined that saying at the dawn of time and has been repeating it to all His "helpers" since. We have many examples in scripture detailing the rescue efforts God was forced to make when His "helpers" got impatient or frustrated with what God was doing, or apparently to them not doing quickly enough. Whenever anyone tried to help God, it was soon discovered God did not especially need a helper.

Mary modeled the behavior we should adopt when God tasks us with an impossible for us to do without Him favor. Mary went to visit her cousin and got involved in God's plan for Elisabeth's life. Mary purposely distracted herself from frustration or growing impatient by doing something else while waiting for God's plan for her to reach full term. In essence Mary removed herself from the equation of pregnancy and devoted herself to the pregnancy of Elisabeth.

God has a plan for each of His children. It is a grand plan, to be sure. When we try to aide that plan in its realization, more often than not, we mess it up. It is best if we find something else to do while God 'incubates' the plan He has for us to fulfill. Take a clue from Mary. Mary went to a personal relation, someone she knew, her cousin Elisabeth, who was going through a very similar experience. They were both pregnant and Mary began to serve Elisabeth in order to make Elisabeth's "God-plan" successful and prosperous. When Elisabeth gave birth to John the Baptist, Mary peacefully transitioned to the next phase of God's plan, which culminated in the birth of our Lord Jesus Christ. When we chill out, God's will fills out.

When we see the beginnings of God's plan start to unfold before us that is the time we need to mindfully, purposefully make our God larger in our lives. Mary magnified God. To magnify something is to make it larger than it currently appears. Realistically, people cannot make God any bigger than He already is-He is God all by Himself! But what we often do is stop God from being big in our personal lives. We get bogged down in the details and pace of existence and God gets smaller and smaller-is less and less important and relevant-until we are left wondering if He is even in our lives at all.

Mary did not wait for an emergency or a crisis to cry out to God and make him ever larger in her life. She started magnifying God-making Him bigger-on a happy day marked by Mary being reunited with her cousin and celebrating the shared joy of impending babyhood. By starting the process of increasing the size and importance of her God at her conception, Mary laid a foundation of God's presence in her life that would carry her beyond the cross on which she saw her son die. Mary, like the other disciples at the time, did not have all the understanding of what was to follow after Jesus said it is finished, but she did not abandon her big God. And thankfully, God did not abandon Mary-just as He won't leave us today.

She accompanied the group of ladies to the tomb to put oils and spices on her son's dead body. There is no record that she cursed God, or railed emotionally at what she had witnessed. The beauty of Mary is her ability to ponder, to think on things and to keep them in her heart. By magnifying God, making Him of larger importance in her life, Mary's capacity to faithfully endure to the end had been solidified in her spirit. If she had only been in it for the fame of birthing the Son of God, she would never have gone to the tomb.

The tomb represented her humiliation, her failure to the prophetic promise of God as she knew it at that moment. The angel had told Mary that the kingdom Jesus would reign over would be without end. Death pretty much ends stuff on earth. That truth was especially painful as Mary approached the tomb of her son. Mary was more invested in Jesus than anyone, except God. She had suffered the indignity of being a tainted woman and she had felt him kick in her womb. She had seen the angels, the shepherds and the wise men all worship this boy. She had watched in silent wonder as he grew up alone and detached from his half-siblings.

Mary had wondered at the wisdom Jesus demonstrated with the leaders of the temple and smiled in motherly pride when people related the miracles attributed to her son. When Jesus rode into Jerusalem to the acclaim of the thronging crowds, imagine the pride and anticipation Mary must have felt when she heard Hosanna's ringing through the streets. A week later, a nightmare began and she watched in tear-streaked horror as her son was unjustly and inhumanely crucified…to death.

Now she was walking to a tomb; his tomb. She should be kneeling before a throne, not a cold slab of stone. For her, in that capsule of time, there was no more son, there was no salvation, there was no messiah, and there was no everlasting kingdom. There was only the stink of death and the perfume she was carrying would only cover that stench for a short time.

The saving grace for Mary is that she had begun to make God bigger than her understanding from day one of her Jesus journey. Mary magnified God-made Him larger-in her life. Every day God occupied more space in Mary's life than He had the previous day. That principle is what gave her the strength to go to a tomb on the day of what appeared to be total defeat.

It is difficult for a person to consciously make God big in any aspect of thought, action, or even life, at the last possible minute, in the middle of crisis. Too many things are in competition for the attention necessary for survival. God must be big in the good day, in the high moments in order for peace to overcome torment. Learn to magnify God in the moments when He already seems big and in control, so that when life seems out of control, He is there already, you won't have to dredge Him up from the dark corner of the place you've hidden Him.

Make the God of the universe, the God of creation, the God of everything, the biggest, most magnified presence in your life every day. Each and every day purposefully magnify-enlarge and make clearer-your God, the God of gods, especially on the good days. If you do this, you will find that in the bad days, He has not left or forsaken you, God is right where you have placed Him, front and center.

The something about Mary is her intuitive understanding of God's sovereignty and majesty and her role as a co-laborer with God in fulfilling His plan for humanity. Mary accepted God's favor and in turn did a favor for God that blessed all humankind for an eternity. Mary asked questions which helped her understand how she could help in the success of God's plan. Mary agreed to work with God as His servant, or surrogate and He overshadowed her with His enduring, powerful presence.

Mary didn't try to assist God unnecessarily, but served another person who was further along in a personal God-plan than Mary was in hers. When the timing was right, Mary moved on with God. Most importantly, Mary magnified and personalized her God, so that when trials came, she had the power to remain faithful to the end and beyond.

Make the something about Mary the something about you, too. Six principles that will make the world you live in take notice of the God who lives in you;

> Accept God's blessing of favor!
> Ask the right question!
> Take encouragement from what God is doing for others now!
> Say yes to God!
> Go on vacation!
> Make your God bigger!

The day is coming when God will reveal the something about you to the world! Be blessed and let the adventure of your life begin today!

Concluding Remarks

Although this book is written to detail the 'something' about Mary to a Christian audience who may be more familiar with the Biblical themes contained within it, my hope is that non-Christian readers will enjoy it and learn from it, as well. If that hope materializes, it will ultimately bring those who have never made a decision to follow the Man, Jesus Christ–the Son of God–to eternal cross-roads.

The first and fourth truths revealed in the 'something' about Mary are where those individuals who have yet to follow Christ must begin today. Accept the blessing of God's favor and seize the opportunity He is presenting to you right now. You might be asking, "How do I do this"? I am thrilled that you asked.

The Bible tells us that it is God's goodness which leads men people to follow Him (Romans

2:4). His goodness is revealed in that while we were still in sin, Christ died to forgive and redeem us and to bring us into right standing and good relations with God (Ephesians 2:4-7). God is not looking to condemn mankind to an eternity apart from Him. He has made every sacrifice and taken every effort to adopt all people as sons and daughters in the family of God. That is the very definition of favor-someone doing something for you, even when you don't deserve it, haven't earned it, and don't realize its priceless value.

God did that for us by sacrificing His own Son as payment for our sin-debt. Jesus was rejected by God, so we could be accepted and favored by Him. Jesus became the sin sacrifice for mankind so we could live in righteous relationship with God. The very God of peace wants to live in us by His Holy Spirit, and His Son made that prospect possible.

That leads us to the fourth truth of the 'something' about Mary. Today is the day when you can seize the opportunity God is presenting to you as you read this book. Accept the favor of God by seizing the opportunity of God's salvation through His Son, Jesus Christ. Today is your day to enter the kingdom of God by the Spirit of God. The Bible tells us that if we believe in our hearts that God has raised Jesus from the dead and confess (speak) with our mouths that Jesus is Lord, then we will be saved (Romans 10:9,10). It may seem simple, but it is in reality very profound.

If you have never made Jesus the Lord of your life, you can do so today. The 'something' about Mary can be activated in you and you can begin to live the adventure God has planned for you with His Spirit directing you in every situation or circumstance you encounter. If you would like to make Jesus the Lord of your life, then read the following prayer, ask God to forgive you and help you live for Him from this day forward.

> Dear Heavenly Father, I know you desire for me to live in your favor forever. I believe you raised Jesus from the dead after He died for my sins. Jesus paid for my sins by shedding His blood for me and today I ask Him to be the Lord of my life. Jesus, you are my Lord and Savior. I thank you for for-giving me from all my sins and adopting me into your family. With

the help of your Holy Spirit, I will live for you from this day forward.

I pray this in the name of your Son, Jesus.

Amen

If you said that prayer, the next steps for you are to find a place where you can meet regularly to receive more training from the Bible. Find a local church where the Bible is taught, where you can become friends with other believers and where you can become involved in serving and assisting others.

Live to let the world see the 'something' in you!

CPSIA information can be obtained
at www.ICGtesting.com
Printed in the USA
BVOW11s1421080316

439498BV00006B/11/P

9 781498 403580